THE LITTLE GOLDEN

ABCDEFGHIJKLMNOPQRSTUVWXYZ

Pictures by

Cornelius DeWitt

GOLDEN PRESS • NEW YORK

Western Publishing Company, Inc., Racine, Wisconsin

Forty-fifth Printing, 1982

A a a

airplane

apple

alligator

auto

ant

B b *b*

ball

bee

bear

butterfly

boy

boat

C c c

clown

cowboy

cow

cock

chair

camel

cat

D d d

duck

deer

drum

donkey

doll

doll house

dog

E e e

egg

Eskimo

elephant

G g *g*

giraffe

gingerbread man

goose

girl

goat

H h h

hat

horse

house

I *i*

iris

iron

iceberg

jam

jar

jack-o'-lanter

juggler

J *j*

jack-in-the-box

K ^kₖ

kite

kitten

knife

key

lollipop

lamp

L l

lion

mittens

monkey

mouse

milk

M m

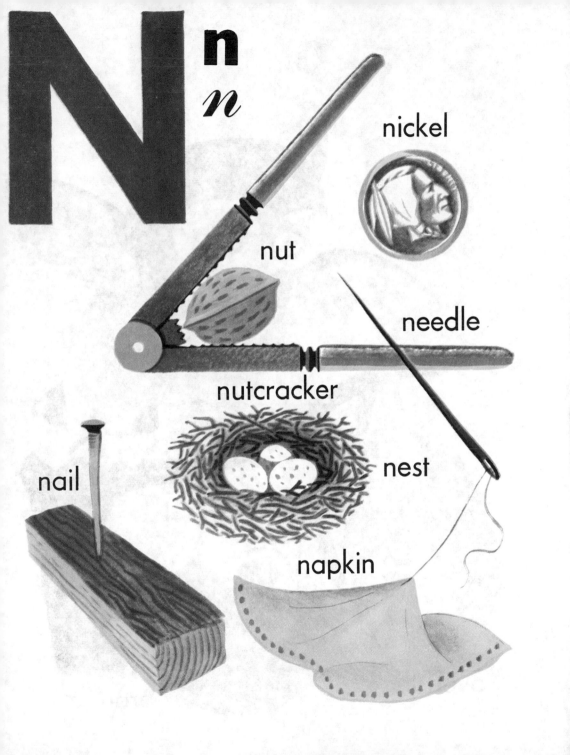

owl

overalls

orange

P p

parrot

pig

pony

pad   pencil

pan

pail

plum

peach   pear

policeman

Q q q

queen

quail   quilt

R r

rake

robin

ring

raccoon

rabbit

rattle

rooster

raven

raft

S s

spider

spoon

squirrel

sheep

seal

sofa

sea horse

shrimp

snake

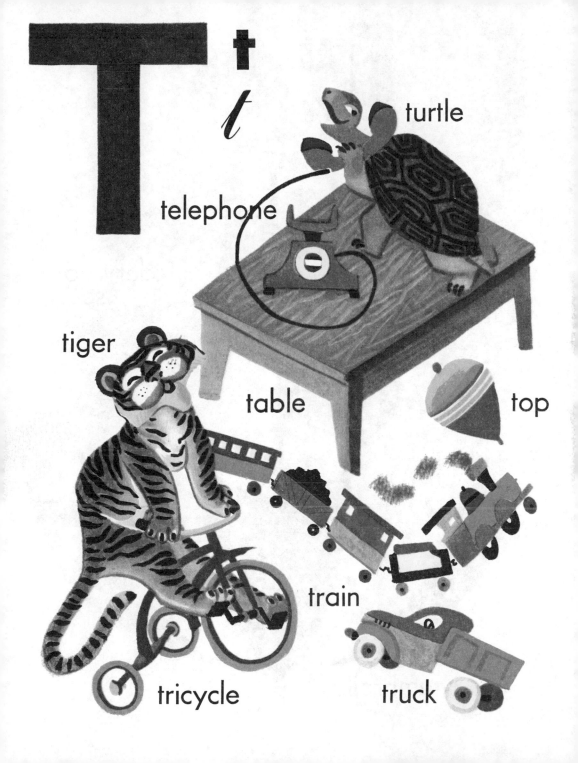

T t

turtle

telephone

tiger

table

top

train

tricycle

truck

U u *u*

underwear

umbrella

V v

violets

veil

violin

vase

valentine

W W w

wolf

walrus

wagon

watermelon

worm

wheel

wheelbarrow

X x

xylophone

yak

yarn

Y y

ZOO